Contents

Note

Christians number years as either BC ('Before Christ') or AD ('*Anno Domini*' – Latin for 'In the year of our Lord'). In this book, however, years are described as being either BCE ('Before the Common Era') or CE ('Common Era').

Introduction

Christianity began about two thousand years ago when a man called Jesus was alive. Jesus lived in the town of Nazareth in a small Middle Eastern country. He worked as a carpenter until he was thirty. Then he spent three years wandering around the country and teaching.

Jesus travelled to the city of Jerusalem. There, he was arrested and put to death by **crucifixion**. This meant that Jesus died nailed to a cross.

▼ *This map shows the parts of the world where Christians live today. Catholic, Protestant and Orthodox traditions are all types of Christianity.*

weblinks

For ideas about where to look for more information about Christianity, go to www.waylinks.co.uk/series/religiontoday/Christianity

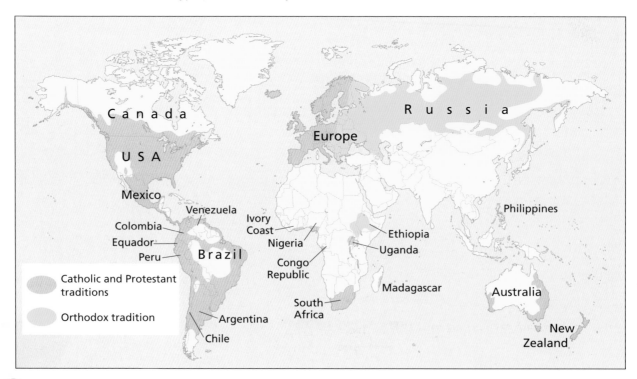

Christianity

Kathryn Walker

WAYLAND

First published in 2007
by Wayland

Wayland
338 Euston Road
London NW1 3BH

Wayland Australia
Level 17/207 Kent Street
Sydney, NSW 2000

Produced for Wayland by Discovery Books
Consultant: Jane Clements, The Council of Christians and Jews
Maps and artwork: Peter Bull

British Library Cataloguing in Publication Data

Walker, Kathryn
    Christianity - (World religions today)
    1. Christianity - Juvenile literature
    I. Title
    294.3

ISBN-13: 978 0 750 2 5263 8

Printed in China
Wayland is a division of Hachette Children's Books,
an Hachette Livre UK company

The publisher would like to thank the following for permission to reproduce
their pictures: Corbis/Kazuyoshi Nomachi cover, The Art Archive 11
Niedersachsisches Museum, 13 Archaeological Museum Spalato/Dagli Orti
(A); Bridgeman Art Library www.bridgeman.co.uk/Galleria dell' Accademia,
Florence, Italy 8, Stapleton Collection, UK 9, Bibliotheque Municipale,
Moulins, France/Lauros/Giraudon 17, Sant' Apollinare Nuovo, Ravenna,
Italy/Giraudon 18, National Library, St Petersburg, Russia 21, Hotel Dieu,
Beaune, France/Paul Maeyaert 41; Corbis/Vatican Pool/epa 14; Robert
Harding Picture Library/ J.P. De Mann 7, J. Greenberg 16, Travel Library
30, M. Jenner 31, ASAP 32, R. Francis 33, I. Talby 34, N. Wheeler 35, S.
Grandadam 37, B. Barbier 43; Hutchison Picture Library 40; Alex Keene
25; Ann and Bury Peerless 24, 29; Rex Pictures Ltd/Ilyas J. Dean; Topfoto
19, 20, 22, 23, 26, 27, 28, 38, 39, 44, 45

weblinks

You don't need a computer to use this book. But, for readers who do have access to the Internet, the book provides links to recommended websites which offer additional information and resources on the subject.

You will find weblinks boxes like this on some pages of the book.

weblinks

For more information about a specific topic here, go to www.waylinks.co.uk/series/religiontoday/Christianity

waylinks.co.uk

To help you find the recommended websites easily and quickly, weblinks are provided on our own website, **waylinks.co.uk.** These take you straight to the relevant websites and save you typing in the Internet address yourself.

Internet safety

↗ Never give out personal details, which include: your name, address, school, telephone number, email address, password and mobile number.

↗ Do not respond to messages which make you feel uncomfortable – tell an adult.

↗ Do not arrange to meet in person someone you have met on the Internet.

↗ Never send your picture or anything else to an online friend without a parent's or teacher's permission.

↗ If you see anything that worries you, tell an adult.

A note to adults
Internet use by children should be supervised. We recommend that you install filtering software which blocks unsuitable material.

Website content

The weblinks for this book are checked and updated regularly. However, because of the nature of the Internet, the content of a website may change at any time, or a website may close down without notice. While the Publishers regret any inconvenience this may cause readers, they cannot be responsible for the content of any website other than their own.

WAYLAND

Jesus today

People who follow Jesus' teachings are called Christians. There are about 2,000 million Christians in the world today.

Christians believe that God became a human being and lived on earth as Jesus. This is why Christians call Jesus the Son of God. They also call him '**Christ**' and 'the **Messiah**'. Both these words mean 'the chosen one'.

Christian belief

Jesus died on a cross. Christians believe that three days later he rose from the dead. His followers saw him and touched him.

After 40 days, Jesus returned to heaven. Then God sent his Holy **Spirit** to earth. The Holy Spirit is God's power. It gives strength to people who follow Jesus' teachings.

➤ *These are young Christians in Pakistan. They are taking part in a procession (parade) to mark the day of Jesus' crucifixion.*

Worship

Most Christians worship together in **churches**, chapels or **cathedrals**. Their holy book is the Bible. It is made up of two parts. These are called the **Old** and **New Testaments**.

Christians believe in God the Father, God the Son (Jesus) and God the Holy Spirit. One of the most important parts of being a Christian is to love God and each other. This is what Jesus taught.

1 The growth of Christianity

Christianity began with one man in a small country. Now it has followers throughout the world. Christians have many differences, but they all believe in the same Jesus Christ. They all try to follow his teachings.

Jesus the man

Historians agree that Jesus really did exist. Almost everything we know about him was written by his followers. So what do we know about Jesus?

Jesus was a **Jew**. His father on earth was Joseph and his mother was Mary. Jesus was born in the town of Bethlehem near Jerusalem. But he grew up in Nazareth. This was a town in a region called Galilee.

Jesus went regularly to the local synagogue. A synagogue is a Jewish place of worship. Jesus sometimes read and preached at the synagogue.

➤ *The region where Jesus spent his life is sometimes called 'the Holy Land'. It now lies mainly in Israel, Jordan and in areas controlled by the Palestinian National Authority.*

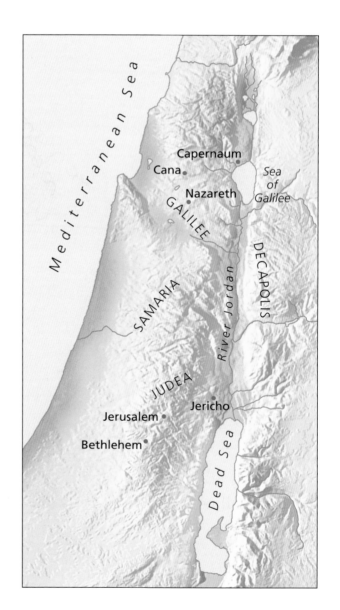

Miracles

*A **miracle** is an event that cannot be explained by science. The New Testament describes many miracles performed by Jesus. Some involved curing blind and dumb people.*

Some Christians have questioned whether these miracles really happened. But many believe they did and that miracle cures can still happen.

◄ *This picture shows the young Jesus in his mother's arms. It is from a church in Ethiopia, Africa.*

Jesus the teacher

When he was about thirty, Jesus chose twelve men to be his closest followers. These men are known as Jesus' **disciples**. Jesus spent three years travelling with them.

Jesus talked to the people they met and taught them. He became very popular. Large crowds came to listen to him. Some brought disabled or sick people. Jesus cured many of them.

Some religious leaders disagreed with what Jesus taught. Others feared he was too popular and might be a threat to the Roman rulers. Some of these men planned to get rid of Jesus.

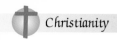
Palm Sunday

Jesus spent three years teaching and healing people. Then he went to Jerusalem. He entered the city riding on a donkey.

Large crowds welcomed Jesus. They cheered and waved branches of palm trees. This is now known as Palm Sunday. It took place five days before Jesus' death.

Every day, Jesus taught at the Temple in Jerusalem. This was the Jews' most holy building.

The Last Supper

On the Thursday evening, Jesus had a special 'last supper' with his disciples. Jesus told them to eat bread and drink wine in his memory. Today, Christians share bread and wine when they take part in the service called Holy Communion.

After supper, Jesus and his disciples went into a garden to pray. The chief **priests** sent soldiers after him.

weblinks

For more information about Christianity, go to www.waylinks.co.uk/series/religiontoday/Christianity

◄ *This picture shows the Last Supper. It was painted in about 1340 by an Italian artist named Taddeo Gaddi.*

They arrested Jesus and took him away. Christians call this day Maundy Thursday.

Good Friday

The chief priests said that Jesus had spoken against God. They sent Jesus to the Roman who controlled the area. His name was Pontius Pilate. Pilate ordered that Jesus be beaten and then nailed to a cross to die.

After he died, Jesus' body was put into a small cave. These things happened on the day Christians call **Good Friday**.

Resurrection

Early on the Sunday morning, a group of women went to the cave. They found it empty. Over the next forty days Jesus appeared to some of his followers.

Christians believe that Jesus returned from the dead. They call this his **Resurrection**. Christians believe that this means they can also live forever in heaven.

➤ *This is a painting of the crucifixion. Jesus was crucified together with two robbers. They are on either side of Jesus. The cross has become a sign of the Christian faith.*

Pentecost

The disciples met seven weeks after the Resurrection. As they prayed together, they heard a sound like rushing wind. Tongues of fire seemed to appear on their heads.

Jesus had promised the disciples that God would send them his Holy Spirit. This would give them strength. The tongues of fire were a sign that this had come true. The disciples began telling people about Jesus. This day is called **Pentecost**.

After this, the disciples became known as '**apostles**'. The word means 'sent out as messengers'.

The Apostle Paul

Religious leaders in Jerusalem tried to stop the apostles teaching people, or preaching, about Jesus. A Jewish man named Saul helped to find and punish Christians.

A few years after Jesus' death, Saul travelled to the city of Damascus. Jesus appeared to him during his journey. Saul became a Christian and changed his name to Paul.

Paul travelled to other countries to spread the teachings of Jesus. He spread Christianity to many places. Paul was finally put to death in Rome because of his beliefs.

Paul's journeys

Journey	Year (CE)	Destination
First	46-47	What is now southern Turkey and Cyprus
Second	50-52	Turkey (then known as Asia Minor) and Greece
Third	52-56	Many of the places he visited on his first two journeys
Final	60	To Rome, as a prisoner

→ Paul's first journey
→ Paul's second journey
→ Paul's third journey
→ Paul's journey to Rome

Paul wrote many letters to the people he had met on his travels. The letters are known as **Epistles**. They form part of the Bible's New Testament.

▼ *This 15th-century painting is of Saul on his journey to Damascus. It shows Jesus appearing to him.*

The spread of the Gospel

The word **Gospel** means 'good news'. It is often used to mean the teachings of Jesus. Christians began to teach the Gospel in countries outside the land where Jesus lived.

Christianity spread through the **Roman Empire**. This was the name for the group of countries controlled by ancient Rome. By the year 300CE it stretched from Spain in the west to Jerusalem in the east (see map).

There were four main centres of Christianity at about this time. These were the cities of Jerusalem, Antioch, Rome and Constantinople.

▼ *This map shows where Christianity had spread to by 300CE. It also shows how strong Christianity was in those places.*

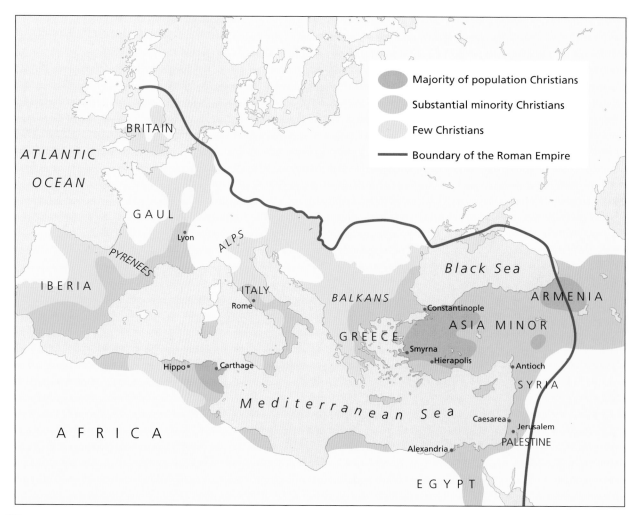

Christians refused to worship the Roman gods and emperors. Because of this, the Romans killed many Christians. Some were crucified or fed to the lions. But Christianity still continued to spread.

Constantine became Emperor of Rome in 312CE. He made Christianity the religion of the Roman Empire (see box below). In the following centuries, Christianity began to spread through Europe.

Emperor Constantine

In 312CE Constantine fought a battle to become Emperor of Rome. The night before the battle, Jesus appeared to him in a dream. Jesus promised that Constantine would win if he fought under the Christian sign of the cross.

The next day, Constantine's army fought with crosses on their shields. They won the battle easily.

Under Constantine's rule, Christians were free to worship. He gave the Roman Empire a new Christian capital. This became known as Constantinople. Today it is the city of Istanbul in Turkey.

▲ *This is a carving on the coffin of Constantine. It shows Constantine holding the Christian cross.*

Divisions in the family

Christians in different countries began to believe slightly different things. The differences grew between the Christian churches of Rome and Constantinople.

In 1054 the Christian Church split into two. In the west it became the **Roman Catholic Church**. In the east it became the **Orthodox** Church. Orthodox Churches are found in Greece, Russia and in other eastern European countries.

Church

The word 'church' has three meanings. It can mean all Christians everywhere. It also means an organized group of Christians, such as the Roman Catholic Church or the Baptist Church. A church is also the word for the building where Christians gather to worship.

▼ *Pope Benedict XVI delivers his first Easter message to crowds gathered in St Peter's Square in Rome. He became pope in 2005.*

Catholic Church

The first leader or **bishop** of Christians in Rome was the apostle Peter. Since Peter, the bishop of Rome has been known as the **Pope**. He is head of the Catholic Church.

The Roman Catholic Church became very powerful. The Pope often told kings and queens how they should rule. Some people began to think that the Church was too powerful and too wealthy.

The Reformation

In the 1500s, there were people who wanted to change, or 'reform' the church. They included a Frenchman called John Calvin and a German called Martin Luther. The quarrel between reformers and the Church led to wars and more division.

This time of fighting and change is known as the **Reformation**. Those who left the Roman Church were called **Protestants**. In England the Church was reformed, but kept some Catholic ways. It is called the Church of England or **Anglican Church**.

weblinks

For more information about the Roman Catholic and Anglican churches, go to www.waylinks.co.uk/series/religiontoday/Christianity

The family of Christian churches

This diagram shows the family of Christian churches. If you follow the arrows, you can see how the Church has divided into different groups over the centuries. Not all Christian groups are shown.

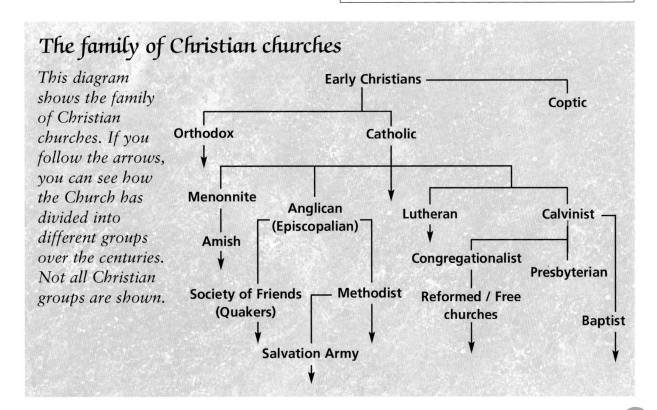

2 Christian beliefs and teachings

For many Christians the Bible is at the centre of their beliefs. This is particularly true for Protestants. For others, what the Church teaches is just as important.

The Christian Bible

The Christian Bible is in two parts. It contains the complete Jewish Bible. Christians call this section the Old Testament. It is made up of 39 separate books. They include histories, rules, songs and stories.

The second part of the Bible is the New Testament. This is made up of 27 books. All of them were written in the hundred years after Jesus died.

▼ *Two teenage Christians study the Bible together. They are from New Jersey in the United States.*

The New Testament

The first four books in the New Testament are called the Gospels. They tell us all we know about the life of Jesus.

The Gospels are written by Matthew, Mark, Luke and John. Some people believe that Matthew and John were two of Jesus' disciples (followers).

Luke also wrote the next New Testament book called The Acts of the Apostles. This describes the early years of the Church.

Other books contain Epistles. These are letters written by Paul and other apostles to groups of Christians.

The last book of the New Testament is called the Revelation of **St (Saint)** John. It tells how God will finally put right all the wrongs and troubles of the World.

▼ *Before printing was invented, Christians handwrote copies of the Bible. They often decorated them with pictures of Bible stories. This page is from a 900-year-old Bible. It shows the Bible's account of God creating the world.*

The teachings of Jesus

Jesus taught many things. One was that God favours the poor, not the rich.

Ideas like this were new and very different. This was one reason why large crowds came to listen to Jesus. It was also why some rulers felt threatened by Jesus' teachings.

The four Gospels contain many of Jesus' teachings. Matthew writes about the **Sermon** on the Mount. This was when Jesus spoke on a mountainside to a large crowd. In this sermon, Jesus taught that trying to live a good life is part of loving God. This includes 'loving your neighbour'. It also means loving and forgiving your enemies.

Parables

A listener once asked Jesus 'Who is my neighbour?' Jesus answered by telling a story.

The story was about a Jew who had been robbed and injured. The injured man lay at the roadside. Two men

▼ This 6th-century picture is from a church in Ravenna, Italy. It shows Jesus preaching his Sermon on the Mount.

➤ This painting is by the Dutch artist Vincent van Gogh. It shows the Samaritan helping the injured Jew. The Samaritan lifts the man onto his own horse to take him to an inn.

passed by and did not help him. Then a man from Samaria came. This Samaritan helped the Jew even though Jews disliked Samaritans.

At the end of the story Jesus asked which man had been 'a good neighbour' to the injured man. Jesus told many other stories like this. They are called **parables**. They helped his listeners to understand and remember what he taught.

In our own words

"When I was young, I liked being told stories about Jesus. They sounded nice. Now I'm older, I've found that some of the things Jesus said are quite hard to do."

"Jesus said we should love our enemies. But when someone has said something cruel about me, I find it very hard to forgive them."

The teachings of the Church

Paul's letters, or Epistles, are part of the Bible. In them, Paul taught that Jesus was God made human.

He also taught that Jesus paid for all the bad things that people had done. He paid by suffering and dying on the cross. This made it possible for those who believe in Jesus to be with God when they die.

In one letter, Paul lists the three most important things for Christians. These are to believe in God, to hope and to love generously without looking for reward. He says that the greatest of these three is love.

The Trinity

Later, the Church taught that God has shown himself to humankind in three ways.

◄ *This picture is from a 15th-century prayer book. It shows Jesus rising from the dead. In the background an angel is shown bringing the news to some of Jesus' followers.*

- He is God the Father
- He lived on earth as God's Son, Jesus
- He still lives in the world as the Holy Spirit

The idea that God exists in three ways but is one Being is known as the Trinity.

Holy letters

Paul's Epistles (letters) are not the only ones in the New Testament. There are also some short Epistles. These are said to be written by other followers of Jesus, such as the apostles James, Peter and John.

Creeds

As time went by, the Church tried to make sure all Christians believed the same things. To do this the Church wrote **creeds**.

A creed states the things that people believe. Creeds were read out by people when they became Christians. Today Christians repeat them during church services.

The Apostle's Creed is said by Catholics and Protestants. It begins with the words:

*'I believe in God, the Father Almighty,
creator of heaven and earth.'*

➤ *Many artists have used a dove as a sign of the Holy Spirit. This picture is taken from a 600-year-old French service book.*

3 Private and public worship

Christians believe God is with them at all times. This means that they can pray anywhere. However, Christians have always met to worship God. They also meet to learn more about their faith.

Private prayer

For Christians, prayer means listening and talking to God. Many believe that God 'talks' to them. He does not do this in a voice everyone can hear. Instead he does it by giving them a strong feeling that they should do a particular thing.

▼ *An American Christian family thank God for food before starting their Thanksgiving dinner.*

Many Christians try to say prayers each morning or evening. Some families pray together before a meal. For Christians, prayer means:

• Praising God for his greatness
• Thanking God for gifts such as food and health
• Asking for his help for other people
• Asking for help for yourself.

Some Christians use books of prayers when they pray. Many just talk to God in their own words.

The Lord's Prayer

In the Sermon on the Mount, Jesus taught a prayer that all Christians should say regularly to God. This is called the Lord's Prayer. It is also known as the 'Our Father' because these are its first two words.

Like most Christian prayers, it ends with 'Amen'. This is a Hebrew word meaning 'So be it'. Hebrew is the language of the Jewish people.

In our own words

"I try to say my prayers every evening. I like to say thank you for any good things that have happened. I also say sorry for anything I've done wrong. I ask God to help me. I believe he hears and answers my prayers. He does not always answer them how I want. So I have to trust he knows best."

▼ *Many early prayer books were illustrated with pictures and decorated with beautiful letters. This one was made in the 15th century.*

Places of worship

The first Christians had to meet in secret. This was because it was against Roman law to be a Christian.

After three hundred years, Christians were allowed to worship. They began making special buildings where they could meet and worship. These were called churches.

There are many types of church buildings. Some are very old and some are modern. There are churches with lots of decoration while others are very simple.

Churches are often planned in the shape of a cross. Many have a pointed or square tower at one end. Orthodox churches are usually planned in the shape of a square cross (like a plus sign). They may have a dome in the roof.

Inside a church

The main part of Roman Catholic and Anglican churches is the **altar**. This is a holy table. It is used in the service known as Holy Communion.

There is usually a stand called a lectern where the Bible is read aloud. The **pulpit** is where the priest can

➤ *This is the Church of Our Lady of Health in Bangalore, India. It has a high tower to remind Christians of heaven.*

preach to the people. This is a type of raised platform or stand.

Orthodox churches have a screen that hides the altar. It is covered with holy pictures called icons.

Protestants often call their meeting place a chapel. Preaching and Bible reading are especially important to them. Because of this, the pulpit is usually in the centre of a chapel.

▼ *This is a Russian Orthodox Church in England. Icons (holy pictures) decorate a screen. Through an archway in this screen, the priest can be seen standing at the altar.*

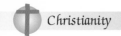

Church leaders

Jesus' disciples were the first leaders of the Church. Today, Church leaders are known by many titles, or names. Those chosen to be leaders must spend several years learning their job.

Catholic, Orthodox and Anglican leaders

Catholic, Orthodox and Anglican Churches have three levels of leaders. These are deacons, priests and bishops. The first level is deacon. After one year, most deacons are made priests. Bishops are senior priests. They are in charge of all the churches in one area. A senior bishop is called an archbishop. He is in charge of the Church for a large area or a whole country.

The Orthodox Church has senior archbishops called patriarchs. In the Roman Catholic Church, some bishops are called cardinals. Cardinals choose who will be Pope.

Protestant Churches

Protestant Churches do not use the word 'priest'. They use the title minister or pastor. The word pastor used to mean shepherd.

weblinks

For more information about the Church of England (the Anglican Church), go to www.waylinks.co.uk/series/religiontoday/Christianity

◄ These men are leaders of the Coptic Church. This is a small part of the Christian Church that was started in Egypt by St Mark. It still uses the an ancient Egyptian language called Coptic.

Monks and nuns

When the Romans finally allowed Christians to worship, some men and women decided to live only for God. They chose to spend their lives in prayer and away from other people. The men became known as monks or friars. The women became known as nuns.

Monks began living together in buildings known as monasteries, while nuns lived in convents. At first, monks and nuns farmed their own land. They spent lots of time praying and studying the Bible.

Today, there are still many monks and nuns. But now they often work in hospitals, schools or nursing homes. They make **vows** (promises) to obey the rules of their monastery or convent.

▼ *Nuns at work in St Joseph's Hospice in Kerala, India. This is a home that cares for people who are dying of cancer.*

Meeting for worship

When Christians worship in church, they believe they are serving God. They also believe that God's Holy Spirit is with them.

Orthodox, Roman Catholics and Protestants have different ways of worshipping. There are even differences within each of these Churches.

Christians usually worship on a Sunday in a church, cathedral or chapel. But worship can take place in the open air or in a home.

Worship includes singing holy songs known as hymns. There is also prayer, readings from the Bible and a sermon. In a sermon, the priest or minister explains part of the Bible.

▲ *Christians in Soweto, South Africa, take part in a service. They give thanks for the blessings they have received.*

Eucharistic worship

Some services carry out Jesus' instruction to remember him by sharing bread and wine (see page 8). This service has different names. It is called the **Eucharist**, Last Supper, Holy Communion or Mass.

The priest or minister says a prayer over the bread and wine. Some Christians see this as a sign of remembering the Last Supper.

Catholics and some others believe that something else happens. They believe that in some mysterious way, the bread and wine actually become the body and blood of Jesus. They believe this although the bread and wine still look and taste the same.

Protestant Churches

One Protestant Church is the Society of Friends. Its members are sometimes called Quakers. They have no priests or prayer books and do not sing hymns. Their meetings are mostly silent prayer and thought.

The Pentecostal Church is another Protestant Church. Their services have lots of joyful singing. Pentecostals believe that miracles can and do happen.

▼ *These worshippers are from southern India. They are waiting to receive Holy Communion.*

Christian art

The first Christians were Jews. They followed the Jewish teaching not to make pictures or statues of holy objects. Over the centuries this changed. Christians began making religious pictures and statues. Many thought that God's church should look as beautiful as possible.

Artists have painted many scenes from the Bible. Sometimes they paint them on church walls and ceilings. For many centuries, ordinary people could not read. These pictures helped them to learn about their religion.

▲ *This is part of the famous painting on the ceiling of the Sistine Chapel in Rome, Italy. It was painted by the artist Michelangelo between the years 1536 and 1541. This section shows God creating Adam (left), the first man.*

At the time of the Reformation (see page 15), many church decorations were destroyed. Protestants felt that they took people's minds away from the word of God. They built simpler churches and chapels.

Music

Singing was an important part of early Christian worship. It still plays an important part in most Christian services today.

Around the year 600CE, Pope Gregory I created the first choir. In the 11th century, an Italian monk invented a way of writing down musical notes.

After the Reformation, Protestants still sang hymns. But they sang without the sound of musical instruments. Later in the 1700s and 1800s, many new hymns were written for Christian church services. Famous composers wrote music for choirs in cathedrals and big churches.

In the 1900s, new types of music became very important in Protestant churches. One type was Black Gospel music. This gives praise to God and teaches the message of the Gospel.

▼ Over the years, Christians paid for many great buildings. This is Durham Cathedral in the northeast of England. Work started in 1093CE and it took forty years to complete.

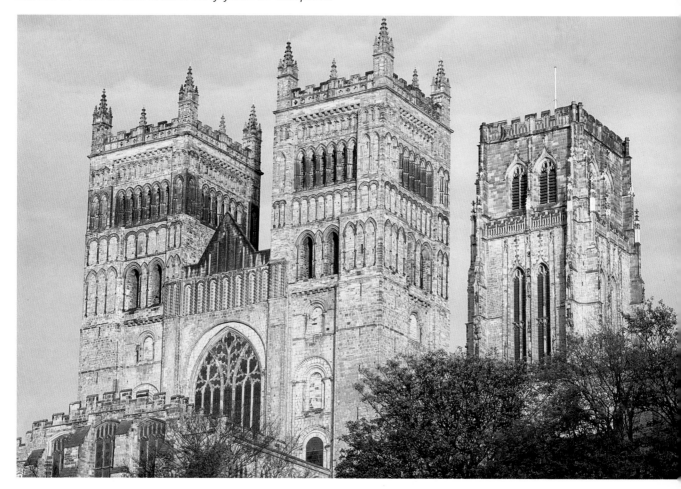

▲ *Roman Catholic priests lead a Christmas service in the Church of the Nativity, near Jerusalem. This church is believed to stand on the exact spot where Jesus was born.*

Festivals

The first Christians celebrated Jesus' Resurrection every Sunday. Soon the Church began to make a special celebration of the Resurrection once a year at **Easter**. It was hundreds of years before Christians made other festivals, such as Christmas.

Christianity spread through the Roman Empire. Christians tried to persuade people to stop celebrating festivals of their old religions. To help them do this, some Christian festivals were celebrated on the same dates as these older festivals.

Christmas

Christmas is when Christians celebrate the birth of Jesus. The date of his birth is unknown. The Church decided to celebrate it on the 25 December. This was the date of the old festival of light.

Easter

The most important Christian festival is Easter. Because it must fall on a Sunday, the date of Easter changes from year to year.

The forty days before Easter is known as Lent. For many Christians this is a time of preparing for Easter and fasting (eating little food).

The week before Easter is known as Holy Week. It begins with Palm Sunday (see page 8). The Friday before Easter is known as Good Friday. This is when special church services remember Jesus' crucifixion.

Ascension and Pentecost

Easter is followed by forty days of rejoicing. Churches are filled with flowers. Then Ascension Day marks the last time Jesus appeared to his disciples.

Ten days later is Pentecost, or Whitsun. This remembers when the Holy Spirit came to the disciples (see page 10).

▼ *Christians carry palm branches through the streets of San Salvador in El Salvador. They do this to remember Jesus entering Jerusalem on the first Palm Sunday.*

4 Living the faith

Christians mark important stages of their lives with special celebrations or services. They also try to love other people, as Jesus taught.

Joining the Church

Christian **baptism** is a service held when a person joins the Church. It is also known as Christening.

The Roman Catholic, Orthodox and some Protestant Churches baptize babies. Baptism takes place at a font. This is usually a large stone bowl inside the church. At baptisms, water is sprinkled on the person's forehead in the sign of the cross.

Baptism

Baptism is also a sign of faith. Some Christians therefore prefer not to

▼ *This baby is being baptized in a Greek Orthodox church in Greece.*

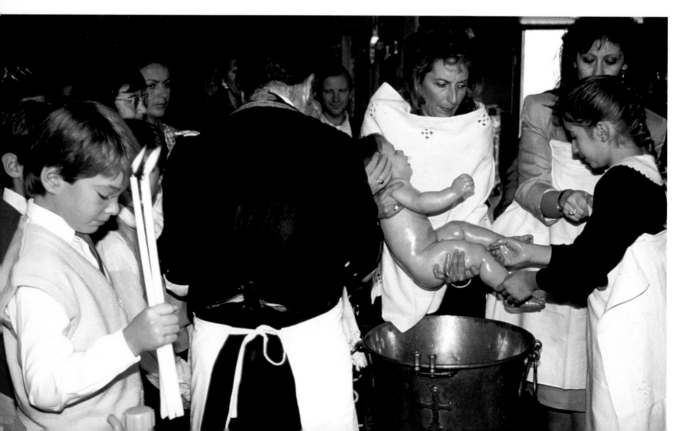

baptize babies because the children do not know what is happening to them. Jesus was baptized when he was an adult.

The Baptist Church only baptizes people who are old enough to understand what they are doing. Then people are plunged into a bath of water for a few seconds. This is a sign that all past sins (wrongs) are being washed away.

John the Baptist

Jesus had a cousin called John who was six months older than him. When John grew up, he lived near the River Jordan. The River Jordan today forms the border between the countries of Israel and Jordan.

Many Jews came to be baptized (or 'washed of their sins') by John in that river. Before he started preaching, Jesus went there to be baptized by John.

Confirmation

Roman Catholic and Protestant churches have a service called **Confirmation**. This is when people become adult members of the Church. A bishop blesses the people being confirmed as full members of the Church.

➤ *Some Christians make a special journey to the River Jordan to be baptized. Jesus was baptized in this river 2,000 years ago.*

Marriage

Christian couples want God's blessing on their marriage, so they usually marry in a church. The man and woman are known as the bride and groom. They make promises or vows to be true to each other in good and bad times.

In Roman Catholic and Anglican Churches, the priest asks if there is any reason in law why the couple should not marry. When the couple have made their vows, he declares them man and wife. Then the priest blesses the marriage.

In some Orthodox churches the couple may wear crowns. This is to show their importance to each other.

Divorce

Most Christians believe that it is best for a couple to marry for life. Jesus taught that marriage brings two people together in a special relationship. He said that divorce is not ideal.

The Orthodox Church has allowed divorce in special cases. The Roman Catholic Church sometimes allows marriages to be annulled. This word means 'made nothing'.

Other Christians feel that if a marriage has failed, it is better for the couple to divorce than to live unhappily. They say that Christianity teaches that we can always have a second chance in life. They then allow people to marry for a second time in church.

Celibacy

Monks and nuns never marry. This is called being celibate. Roman Catholic priests are not allowed to marry, but some people think this may change in the future.

Marriage vows

This is the marriage vow said in an Anglican marriage service:

'I, [name of man/woman] take
you [name of woman/man]
to be my wife/husband
to have and to hold
from this day forward;
for better, for worse,
for richer, for poorer,
in sickness and in health,
to love and to cherish [treat tenderly],
till death us do part,
according to God's holy law:
and this is my solemn vow.'

➤ *This bride and groom are crowned at a Russian Orthodox marriage service.*

▲ *A teenage Christian gives a present to a blind 93-year-old woman. He is also spending time keeping her company.*

Christian action

Christians today still try to follow Jesus' teaching to 'love your neighbour'. They also remember that Jesus said they should help the ill, the hungry and the homeless. This can mean doing good works or fighting for people to be treated fairly.

Neighbourhood help

Many Christians try to help their neighbours every day. This may mean shopping for someone who cannot leave the house. It could be gardening for an old person or visiting a neighbour in hospital.

Many churches organize clubs for elderly and lonely people. Some Christians do voluntary work. This is work that people do without pay.

Giving to charity

All Christians are expected to give some money to their church and to charities. Charities are organizations that collect money and get help for those in need.

Aid to other countries

Many Christian charities work with the poor and needy in their own countries. Others help people in the world's poorest countries. Charities try to provide these people with tools, machinery and money. They also help people to learn new skills.

War

Jesus told his followers to make peace and not to fight. But many battles have been fought in Jesus' name. From the 11th to 13th centuries, Christians fought in the Crusades. These were wars led by European Christians. They tried to win back the Holy Land from Muslims. Muslims are people who follow the faith of Islam.

Some Christians believe that fighting and wars are always wrong. Others think that it is right to go to war if something or someone is very evil or wrong. Then war may be the only way to put it right.

▼ *A charity called Christian Aid set up this scheme in Ethiopia. It helps women earn a living by preparing and selling lentils to local hotels.*

▲ *A burial at Kraal, South Africa. A part of most burial services takes place at the graveside.*

Life everlasting

Christians believe that Jesus has shown that death is not the end. They believe that after death there is life without end. Many think that a part of a person we cannot see lives on. This is called the soul.

Burial

A funeral service can be just a few readings, prayers and hymns. Often the priest or minister will give a sermon about the dead person. Sometimes the funeral is part of a Holy Communion service.

Then the body is buried. This may be in a graveyard by the church or in a cemetery. The prayers said at the graveside are full of hope.

Cremation

Sometimes the body is not buried. Instead it is taken to a special place where the body and coffin is burned in a type of oven, or furnace. This is called cremation. The ashes of the dead person may then be buried or scattered where the family wish.

Heaven and hell

Jesus often spoke about heaven. For Christians, this means the **spiritual** place where God dwells. True believers will be with him after death.

Jesus also spoke of a 'Day of Judgement'. This is when God will decide how well everyone has lived their lives. Some say this will happen when the world ends. Some think it happens for each of us when we die.

Christian Churches used to describe hell as the place where wicked people went after death. It was where they would suffer forever. Today, many Christians feel it is more important to think about God's love and forgiveness. They think 'hell' means being separated from God.

➤ *This 15th century painting is of the Last Judgement. The angel Michael weighs the dead. Some go up to heaven, others go down to hell.*

5 Christianity today

Christianity used to be mainly a European religion. In recent centuries, Christianity has spread to the Americas, Africa and Asia. The Church is now stronger in these areas than it is in Europe.

The Church around the world

From about the year 1850, Christians began travelling in Africa to spread the teachings of Jesus. These people were known as missionaries. Some travelled to China, India and Latin America.

In the United States, Protestant churches became very strong in the 1700s and 1800s. New religions developed that were linked to Christianity, such as the Mormon Church and the Jehovah's Witnesses.

In Europe, big industrial cities were growing. New Christian groups, such as the Salvation Army, preached the Gospel to the city workers. These groups also tried to improve the conditions in which the workers lived.

The 20th century

During the 1900s, the new Churches in Asia, Africa and Latin America grew rapidly. Soon there were far more Christians in these areas than there were in Europe. The biggest growth of Christianity has been seen in Africa.

Number of Christians in Africa	
1950	25 million
1980	100 million
2000	Over 200 million

In the United States Protestant Churches have continued to grow

Fact box

• There are about 2,000 million Christians in the world today.

• Half of all Christians are Roman Catholics.

• There are more non-white Christians than white Christians.

stronger. In the year 2000, 44 per cent of the population said they went to church on Sundays.

In Europe, the number of people going to church grew smaller. By 2000, only about one in ten people go to church on Sundays.

Christians began to feel they should forget their differences. They thought they should work together to spread the teachings of Jesus and do his work. In 1949, the World Council of Churches was formed to help the different Churches do this.

weblinks▸

For more information about the World Council of Churches, go to www.waylinks.co.uk/series/religiontoday/Christianity

➤ *Christians go to a church service in Peru. In South America the majority of Christians are Roman Catholics.*

Christianity now

Jesus told his disciples that the Holy Spirit would come to them. He said that it would give them power to tell people everywhere about him.

Christians believe the Holy Spirit came at the first Pentecost. Since then, Christians have believed they should spread the Gospel by what they say and do.

Christian churches are still doing this today. Christianity is the world's largest religion. It is still growing in countries such as Africa, Russia and China. But in Europe, fewer people than ever are going to church.

▼ *A priest leads the Easter Holy Communion service. This is in an Episcopalian (or Anglican) church in the United States.*

Disagreements

Many people ask why there are so many different Churches and why Christians cannot agree with each other. In the last fifty years, the different Churches have worked and worshipped together more. But they still disagree about many things.

The disagreements are not just between the Churches. People of the same Church disagree with one another. For example, some Roman Catholics believe that women should be allowed to become priests. But their Church says they cannot.

Today it is often easier to think of Christians as being divided into

▲ *Many Christians disagree about abortion. This is when a woman has an operation to end a pregnancy. Some believe abortion is wrong. Others say a woman should be able to choose. Here groups from both sides face each other.*

'traditional' Christians and 'liberal' Christians. Liberal Christians usually think about what Jesus' teachings mean today. They think how best to follow them in the modern world.

Traditional Christians usually believe what the Bible says is true for all time. They think people should not look at the meaning in different ways. Traditional Christians are sometimes called Fundamentalists.

This type of Christianity has become a very powerful force in the United States.

More work to do

Christians have always worked to end suffering. Most realize there is still a lot of work to be done. There are people that still need food and water. There is still disease, poverty and injustice to fight. The Christian story is far from finished.

Glossary

altar The Holy table in a Christian church used for the Eucharist or Holy Communion.

Anglican Church The Church of England and churches in other countries that share its beliefs.

apostles Jesus' closest followers who first spread the teachings of Jesus.

baptism (christening) The ceremony in which a person joins the Church.

bishop The head priest of a particular area.

cathedral The main church in a particular area.

Christ A title in the Greek language meaning 'the chosen one' or 'the anointed one'.

church 1) All Christians, the whole 'family' of believers; 2) A separately organized group of Christians; 3) A building where Christians meet.

Confirmation A service to renew promises made at baptism.

creed A statement of beliefs.

crucifixion Execution by nailing someone to a cross and leaving them there to die.

disciple One of Jesus' closest followers.

Easter The time when Christians celebrate Jesus rising from the dead.

Epistle A letter that forms part of the New Testament.

Eucharist Another name for Holy Communion or the Mass.

Good Friday The day on which Jesus was crucified. It is three days before Easter Sunday.

Gospel ('good news') 1) One of four books about Jesus in the New Testament; 2) The teachings of Jesus.

Jew A member of the Jewish people who follow a religion called Judaism.

Messiah A title in the Hebrew language meaning 'the chosen one' or 'the anointed one'.

miracle An event which cannot be explained by science.

New Testament The collection of Christian writings added to the Old Testament to form the Christian Bible.

Old Testament The Christian name for the Jewish Bible.

Orthodox One of four east European Churches.

parable A short story told to help explain a religous teaching.

Pentecost The day when the Holy Spirit was sent to Jesus' disciples. This happened seven weeks after Easter.

Pope The Bishop of Rome who is head of the Roman Catholic Church.

priest A person who is trained to lead a Christian service in church.

Protestant A member of one of the churches that separated from the Roman Catholic Church in the 16th century.

pulpit A stand in a church from where the sermon is given.

Reformation The change, or reform, of the Roman Catholic Church in the 16th century. This led to Protestant Churches separating from the Roman Church.

Resurrection Jesus' rising from the dead.

Roman Catholic Church The Christian Church based in Rome with the Pope as its head.

Roman Empire The group of countries controlled by ancient Rome.

saint (St) A person who has lived a exceptionally good or holy life and is honoured by the church.

sermon A religious talk given during a church service.

spirit A being without a body.

spiritual To do with the spirit or soul, not the body.

vow A promise.

Timeline

c.7-4BCE	Jesus born
CE	
c.30	Jesus crucified
46-56	Paul makes his three journeys to spread the teachings of Jesus
40-100	Books of the New Testament are written
64-312	The Romans punish Christians for their beliefs
c.100	Christianity has spread around the eastern end of the Mediterranean Sea
312	Christianity becomes the chosen religion of the Roman Empire
597	Christianity brought to Canterbury in southern England
1054	Western (Catholic) and Eastern (Orthodox) Churches split
1517	Martin Luther speaks out against the Roman Catholic Church. This marks the start of the Reformation.
1533	Henry VIII, King of England and Wales, breaks with the Roman Catholic Church. This begins the Church of England.
1850 on	Christian missionaries begin to travel widely in Africa
1900	By now the Bible has been translated into 100 languages
1949	World Council of Churches formed to help Christians work together
2000	Celebrations held to mark 2,000 years of Christianity

Further reading

Easter (Celebrations) by Anita Ganeri (Heinemann Library, 2002)

Great Religious Leaders: Jesus and Christianity by Alan Brown (Hodder Wayland, 2005)

The Lion Treasury of Saints by David Self (Lion Publishing, 2003)

My Christian Year by Cath Senker (Hodder Wayland, 2004)

Religions of the World: Christianity by Sue Penney (Heinemann Library, 2003)

The Roots of the Christian Festivals by David Self (SPCK, 2004)

Index